D0719077

SURVIVING THE

JUNGLE

M. Weber

Copyright © 2019
Published by Full Tilt Press
Written by M. Weber
All rights reserved.

Printed in the United States of America.
No part of this book may be reproduced in any manner whatsoever without written permission,
except in the case of brief quotations embodied in critical articles and reviews.

Full Tilt Press
42982 Osgood Road
Fremont, CA 94539
readfulltilt.com

Full Tilt Press publications may be purchased for educational, business, or sales promotional use.

Editorial Credits
Design and layout by Sara Radka
Edited by Lauren Dupuis-Perez
Copyedited by Kristin Russo

Image Credits
Alamy: Splash News, 34; Getty Images: cover, Bluemoon Stock, 36, deepblue4you, 10, EyeEm, 9, 11, 44, Flickr RF, 31, iStockphoto, 3, 3, 13, 15, 16, 17, 19, 23, 25, 28, 35, 36, 37, 37, 37, 43, 44, Joao Paulo Burini, 3, 21, Matteo Colombo, 27, Moment RF, 33, Zedcor Wholly Owned, 22; Newscom: EFE, 29; Pixabay: background, 1, 2, 3, 5, 38, 39; Wikimedia: Maria or Hans-Wilhelm Koepcke, 7

ISBN: 978-1-62920-741-4 (library binding)
ISBN: 978-1-62920-781-0 (eBook)

full tilt
PRESS

CONTENTS

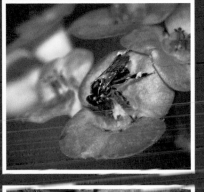

SURVIVING THE JUNGLE

The jungle is one of Earth's most dangerous places. More than 50 percent of the world's plant and animal species live deep in the jungle. Poisonous plants grow in every direction. People who go into the jungle must be prepared to run into many different threats. Trees as tall as buildings loom overhead. Food and water may be hard to find. The thick **canopy** makes it dark on the jungle floor.

What does it take to survive there? To return to civilization, survivors must have an **iron will** to keep going—even when they are scared and far from home.

canopy: the topmost branges of trees in a forest, that form a layer of foliage above the forest floor

iron will: having a strong feeling that you are going to do something and that you will not allow anything to stop you

LONG WAY DOWN

Juliane Koepcke

Peru

10 days

Panguana, a biological research station in Peru, allows volunteers, researchers, and students the chance for hands-on learning. In 1971, Juliane Koepcke and her parents were living there.

"I knew they had stopped searching."

JULIANE KOEPCKE

On Christmas Eve, 1971, Juliane Koepcke was flying through a storm. The 17-year-old lived with her parents. Her parents were German scientists. The family lived in Peru on an environmental **preserve**. The preserve was deep in the jungle. Juliane and her mother had traveled to the city of Lima to celebrate Juliane's graduation from high school. They were traveling home to Juliane's father. After waiting for the delayed plane, they were finally able to take off.

Suddenly, the weather turned dark and stormy. Lightning flashed outside the plane windows. The plane began to shake. Juliane looked at her mother. Her mother was worried. "Now it's over," her mother said. Juliane blacked out as the plane split apart. She fell toward the jungle below.

preserve: an area where wildlife or natural resources are protected

ALIVE BUT LOST

Juliane woke up in the jungle. She was on the ground near her airplane seat. Her watch said that it was close to nine a.m. It was Christmas morning, and Juliane was all alone in the middle of the Peruvian jungle. Juliane knew a lot about the jungle. Her parents had taught her important information about surviving. Once she could walk again, Juliane first searched for her mother. However, her mother had not survived the crash.

Juliane moved slowly through the jungle, using one of her shoes to pat the ground in front of her. This way, she could check for snakes. Planes circled overhead, looking for the wreckage. "But I couldn't draw their attention to me, and after a while, I didn't see them above me anymore, and that's when I knew they had stopped searching." The search planes couldn't see Juliane through the thick canopy. Juliane needed to get out of the jungle by herself.

The rain forest canopy is about 20 feet (6 meters) thick. It is made up of many layers of tree branches, leaves, and the animals that live there.

SHELTER AND RESCUE

When Juliane found a river, she was able to walk in the water. This was safer than walking on dry ground. It is harder to see snakes, spiders, and other dangers on dry land. One large cut on her arm was infected. **Maggots** were in the wound. Maggots are dangerous. They can cause an infection to grow.

After 10 days of walking through the jungle, Juliane found a boat. She used the gasoline from the motor to clean out the maggots from the cut on her arm. There was a shack near the boat. Juliane was weak and decided to stay in the shack to rest. The next day, three men appeared outside. She said when she heard them, "It was like hearing angels' voices." At first they were frightened of her. She had been in the jungle more than a week and had survived a plane crash. The men thought she looked like a ghost. She told them what had happened to her. They took her down the river in their boat to a small hospital. After some treatment, she was flown back to her father.

WINGS OF HOPE

In 2000, a famous director named Werner Herzog made a documentary about Juliane's experience. The movie was called *Wings of Hope*. For the first time, Juliane returned to the area where she had been lost. She shared her experience and memories for the film.

maggot: a small insect that looks like a worm; the young form of a fly

Finding a shelter is one of the most important steps to surviving in the rain forest. Experts also suggest wearing waterproof shoes and protecting your skin from bugs.

STARTING LOCATION
Airport in Peru
RESCUE LOCATION
In the jungle at a shack near a river.

VENEZUELA

SURINAME

COLOMBIA

VENEZUELA

FRENCH GUIANA

PERU

BRAZIL

N
W E
S

Lima

BOLIVIA

PARAGUAY

☆ Starting location

☆ Rescue location

CHILE

ARGENTINA

WALKING INTO DANGER

Gileno Vieira da Rocha
Brazil
12 days

The dense jungle makes it very difficult for people to find their way without a clear path.

"I'm so happy it's all over."

GILENO VIEIRA DA ROCHA

Gileno Vieira da Rocha was working with a crew building a road. The road was in a **remote** area of the Amazon in Brazil. The project took place in August 2014. The 65-year-old was staying in a hotel near the worksite. The crew was working 6 miles (10 kilometers) from Apuí, the nearest town. The closest large city was nearly 300 miles (483 km) away.

Gileno got into an argument with other workers staying in the hotel. He decided to walk to Apuí. He wanted to take a shortcut across a field. Unfortunately, it is easy to lose track of direction in the jungle. Gileno walked and walked through the trees and tangled **underbrush**. He was surrounded by plants, insects, and other animals. Soon, Gileno realized he was lost. He did not know how to get out of the jungle.

remote: far from cities or populated areas

underbrush: bushes, small trees, and other plants that grow under a forest's larger trees

NOT PREPARED

Gileno was in a dangerous situation. It is difficult to survive in the jungle even with another person, and Gileno was alone. He had not expected he would get lost. Because he had grown up near the Amazon jungle, he knew that it was possible to survive. He decided to continue walking. This would hopefully lead him back to a town. Gileno needed to find food and water. He knew he could collect rainwater to drink. To eat, he captured bugs and wasps. He looked for larger animals to hunt. All he could catch were flies. It takes about 20 flies to equal the amount of calories of a cheeseburger.

After 12 days of walking, he started to get sick from the heat of the jungle. He suffered from cuts and scrapes on his skin. He still could not find any signs of human activity. During his disappearance, his family never gave up hope that he would be found alive.

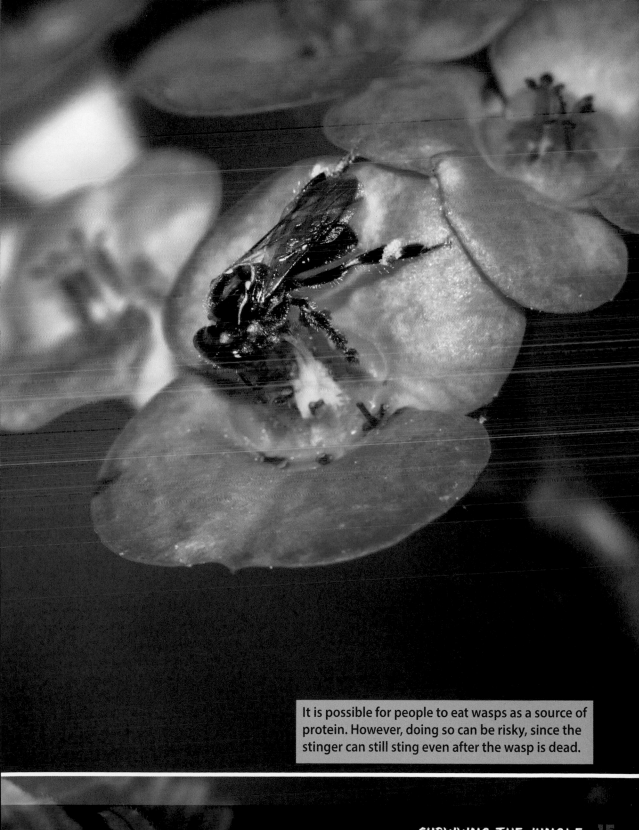

It is possible for people to eat wasps as a source of protein. However, doing so can be risky, since the stinger can still sting even after the wasp is dead.

HAPPY TO BE ALIVE

Gileno knew he was in trouble. He was very weak. He was not always able to stay **conscious** and needed to stop and rest often. When he was unconscious, he was **vulnerable** to the dangers of the jungle. Gileno didn't know it, but a team of rescuers had gone out looking for him. However, it was a man from a local jungle tribe that found Gileno.

Gileno was unconscious next to a river when the man found him. Gileno was less than 10 miles (16 km) from where he had gone missing. When he was rescued he said, "I'm so happy it's all over. Now I want to show my gratitude at being alive by sharing happiness with everyone who knows me." Gileno returned to his family, where he was able to fully recover.

EATING INSECTS

People who are lost in the jungle aren't the only ones who eat insects. More than 1,400 types of insects are regularly eaten around the world. These insects are gathered and prepared for meals. They are often a good source of protein. Insects like worms and termites are easy to find and can be boiled or roasted.

conscious: awake and aware of your surroundings

vulnerable: able to be easily attacked or hurt

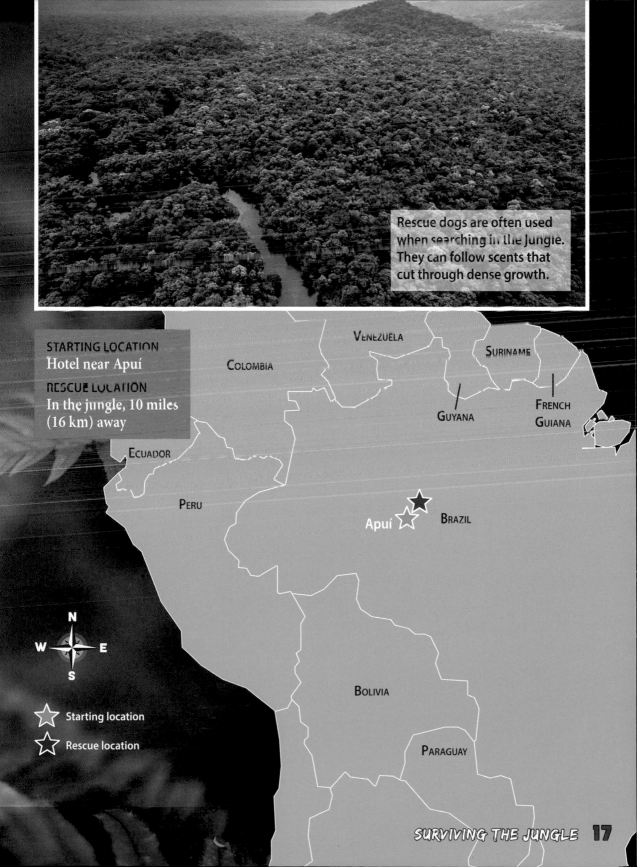

Rescue dogs are often used when searching in the jungle. They can follow scents that cut through dense growth.

STARTING LOCATION
Hotel near Apuí

RESCUE LOCATION
In the jungle, 10 miles (16 km) away

VENEZUELA

COLOMBIA

SURINAME

GUYANA

FRENCH GUIANA

ECUADOR

PERU

Apuí ☆ ★ BRAZIL

N
W E
S

☆ Starting location

☆ Rescue location

BOLIVIA

PARAGUAY

ADVENTURE
OF A LIFETIME

Loïc Pillois
 and Guilhem Nayral
French Guiana
Seven weeks

Poison dart frogs are often very bright colors. This warns other animals to stay away.

"To have found Guilhem at this place is nothing short of a miracle."

THIERRY LE GUEN

Loïc Pillois and Guilhem Nayral were two 34-year-old Frenchmen looking for an adventure in the Amazon. They headed out in February 2007. They wanted to try to survive in the jungle. They would soon learn just how hard it is to live in one of the world's most dangerous environments.

Loïc and Guilhem took a helicopter deep into the jungle. They had enough supplies for two weeks. They wanted to hike from the drop-off point of Grand Kanori Falls to the tiny town of Saül. They had a map to guide them on their journey. All around them were dangerous animals. There were tree frogs that could kill or **paralyze** them with poison. There were giant anaconda snakes.

Due to their inexperience, the two men quickly lost track of where they were. They suddenly realized they were lost and would need to test their survival skills.

paralyze: to make an animal or human unable to move

FOOD AND SHELTER

Loïc and Guilhem were overwhelmed by the difficult **terrain**. Instead of moving deeper into the jungle, they decided to build a shelter. They believed that they might be rescued if they stayed in one place. They also built a fire hoping it would help rescuers find them. When they heard helicopters overhead, they were excited. But the jungle is covered by a thick canopy of trees and plants. The rescuers could not see them.

The two men soon had to find food. They captured two turtles. They also ate centipedes and spiders. This was dangerous. Guilhem became sick from the **venom** in a spider. He also became infested by **parasites** living in his skin. It rained every day and the men were always wet. Loïc knew they would have to travel in order to get help and save his sick friend.

terrain: a particular kind of land

venom: a poison that is inside of certain animals, such as insects and snakes, that can cause harm to humans or other animals

parasite: an animal or plant that lives in or on another animal or plant and gets food or protection from it

The Brazilian wandering spider is one of the most poisonous spiders on the planet. Spiders must be especially well-cooked or they can be dangerous for humans to eat.

GOING AHEAD ALONE

Loïc and Guilhem were in the jungle for seven weeks. The men knew rescue would not be able to find them in their shelter. The rain and tough terrain made surviving harder and harder each day. At first, the two men walked together. Then Loïc realized he needed to find help for Guilhem soon or he could die. He thought they may be close to Saül. Loïc left Guilhem and continued into the jungle alone. He planned to return to his friend as soon as he could.

Loïc reached Saül early in the morning. It was also the day his family reached Saül. His family had traveled from France to help look for the lost men. Loïc sent a rescue team back into the jungle. Four hours later, they found Guilhem. Thierry le Guen, a rescuer, said, "To have found Guilhem at this place is nothing short of a miracle. That forest is as thick as broccoli and the canopy shoots up 40 meters" (131 feet). The two men were treated for their injuries while surrounded by loved ones.

JUNGLE CUISINE

People who live in the jungle must rely on local food sources. Native Amazon tribes eat bird-eating spiders. They are considered a delicacy. The tribes prepare the spiders by roasting the spiders over a fire. They burn and scrape off the hairs of the spiders before eating them.

Anywhere from 50 to 90 percent of plant and animal life found in jungles lives in the trees.

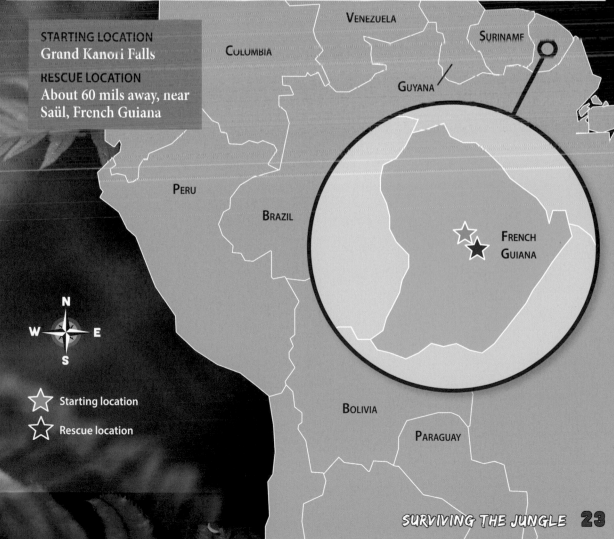

STARTING LOCATION
Grand Kanoi Falls

RESCUE LOCATION
About 60 mils away, near Saül, French Guiana

VENEZUELA

COLUMBIA

SURINAME

GUYANA

PERU

BRAZIL

FRENCH GUIANA

N
W E
S

BOLIVIA

PARAGUAY

⭐ Starting location

⭐ Rescue location

OVER THE EDGE

Yossi Ghinsberg
Bolivia
Three weeks

Spider monkeys have long arms, legs, and tails that can hold onto branches of trees. They mostly live in the rain forests of Central and South America, but can also be found in some parts of Mexico.

"The toughest moment was after a few days, when I realized that I was completely alone."

YOSSI GHINSBERG

In 1981, Yossi Ghinsberg was 22 years old. He had just finished serving in the Israeli military. He was looking for adventure when he traveled to Bolivia. There, he met other young men who wanted to explore the world. They decided to set off as a group. They were going to look for a group of people who lived in the rain forest. They traveled together for a few weeks. They even hunted monkeys to eat.

The men soon disagreed on how to continue. Yossi decided to go with an American man named Kevin Gale. Kevin wanted to build a raft and go down a river. Yossi and Kevin decided to continue down the river on the raft. The other two men set off in a different direction. Just as they approached a waterfall, Yossi and Kevin lost control of the raft. Kevin was able to jump into the water and swim to shore. Yossi found himself falling as the raft went over the waterfall.

THE FIGHT TO LIVE

Falling over the waterfall was like riding a rollercoaster. Yossi was thrilled to reach the shore and survive the fall. However, he was now lost in the Bolivian rain forest. He had some supplies with him, but very little food. He fought off a jaguar attack with a bottle of insect repellent. He was able to light the repellent on fire to scare away the giant cat.

He found fruit to eat. He traveled near the river, hoping it would lead him to rescue. It rained often. Soon, the area started to flood. It was very dangerous. "The toughest moment," Yossi remembered, "was after a few days, when I realized that I was completely alone." For two days, he felt a woman walking with him, giving him encouragement. Even today he does not know if the woman was real or his imagination. "It was no less of a miracle if it was my imagination which had summoned her up, because it happened at the very moment I had broken down and given up."

Waterfalls are created over long periods of time. Water moving downstream washes away soft rocks, creating a steep fall.

NOT FORGOTTEN

Yossi thought of the woman as his first miracle. The second miracle was his rescue. Yossi had been lost for three weeks. He was in a lot of pain. There were many cuts on his feet that made walking painful. He did not know how much longer he would be able to keep going. Yossi stopped to rest on the side of the river. That was when a boat approached. As it did, he saw his friend Kevin in the boat. Kevin had made it out of the jungle and was returning in search of Yossi. Kevin had almost given up hope and was looking for a place to turn the boat around. That place ended up being just where Yossi had stopped to rest. Yossi and Kevin remained friends long after they left Bolivia.

JAGUARS

Jaguars are the third-largest cat on Earth, behind lions and tigers. They are the largest cat found in the Americas. Jaguars live and hunt alone. In the jungle, they can climb trees and travel across branches. This makes them dangerous on the ground and from above. They are so powerful that they can kill their prey, such as deer or monkeys, with one crushing bite to the skull.

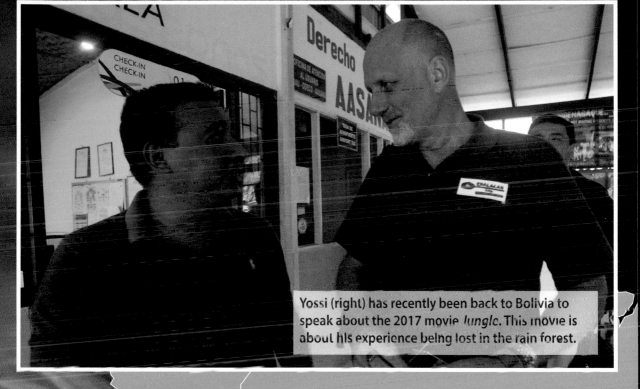

Yossi (right) has recently been back to Bolivia to speak about the 2017 movie *Jungle*. This movie is about his experience being lost in the rain forest.

STARTING LOCATION
Northwest Bolivia (exact location unknown)

RESCUE LOCATION
The Beni River, near Rurrenbaque, Bolvia

BRAZIL

PERU

BOLIVIA

PARAGUAY

 Rescue location

RAISED BY MONKEYS

Marina Chapman
Colombia
Five years

About six percent of the Amazon rain forest is located in Colombia.

"It gives you goosebumps . . . "

MARINA CHAPMAN

Marina Chapman has an amazing story to tell. For many years, she only told the story to close family members and friends. But with their encouragement, she decided to write a book. The book is called *The Girl With No Name*. In it, Marina reveals that when she was a small child, she spent years living in the jungle. During those years, she lived without any human contact. In order to survive, she lived with a group of monkeys.

While not everyone believes her story, Marina says that it is true. Her story begins when she was five years old. During a party, she remembers being taken away by strange men. She doesn't remember who she was before she went missing from her home in Colombia. When her kidnappers abandoned her in the jungle, she walked until she found a group of monkeys. Because they were human-like, she thought they could help her.

WATCH AND LEARN

The monkeys, who are believed to be Capuchins, were not afraid of Marina. Marina was only a small child. She watched what the monkeys did. She was able to look for fruit because she copied the monkeys. At first, she didn't feel like she belonged. But she soon learned how to climb trees like them, and was slowly accepted into their group. One of them even helped her after she ate a piece of fruit that made her sick. One of the oldest monkeys noticed Marina needed help. The monkey led Marina to bad water that would make her throw up. Once she had thrown up, she got better.

After this time, the monkeys accepted Marina. Marina was able to sit in the trees with the monkeys and feel safe. She says they would even **bond** with her. They did this by combing her hair with their fingers, looking for bugs to eat. This is called grooming. She enjoyed the experience, saying, "It gives you goosebumps when they go through your hair and eat the things they find in it."

bond: to form a relationship with someone

Capuchin monkeys are small in size. They weigh between 3 and 9 pounds (1.4 and 4.1 kilograms). They are about the size of a house cat.

LEAVING THE JUNGLE

Marina thinks she spent five years in the jungle. Because she was so young, she does not know for sure how long she lived with the monkeys. One day, she heard hunters in the jungle. Marina had forgotten how to speak, but she knew she wasn't supposed to be living with the monkeys. She approached the hunters and was able to talk through grunts and noises. The men took her to nearby Cucuta, Colombia. Because she did not know who her family was, she was also alone in the city. She worked as a servant. Eventually she was able to learn how to speak again. After surviving on her own, she was adopted by a family in Bogota, Colombia. She grew up and moved to England. After many years of living a successful life, she was able to tell her story by writing a book. She never forgot her time in the jungle and remembers the monkeys fondly.

Marina's daughter, Vanessa, helped her mom tell her story about being raised by monkeys as a child.

CAPUCHIN MONKEYS

Capuchin monkeys are highly social and communicate with complex facial expressions and gestures. These gestures can include poking each other in the eyes. It is a way to show social bonds. Capuchin monkeys are often used in TV shows and movies. They are friendly and will work with people.

STARTING LOCATION
Near the border of Venezuela and Colombia (exact location unknown)

RESCUE LOCATION
Near Cucuta, Colombia

VENEZUELA

SURINAME

COLOMBIA

GUYANA

ECUADOR

PERU

BRAZIL

BOLIVIA

 Rescue location

CONTAINER FOR WATER

Collecting fresh water is vital for survival. This could be a canteen or another container.

INSECT REPELLENT

There are many kinds of insects in the jungle. Insect repellent can help keep bugs away. This means you will have fewer bug bites that may carry disease or get infected from scratching.

SHOES

Shoes are very important in the jungle. Shoes will protect your feet. They should be made of tough material, since you may have miles of walking ahead of you.

MAPS

A map can help explorers find their way in the jungle. Maps can show where rivers are located. Maps can also show how far away towns are.

SHELTER

Bringing some kind of shelter can help save your life. Shelter can protect you from sun and rain. A shelter can include a tent or tarp strung up in the trees.

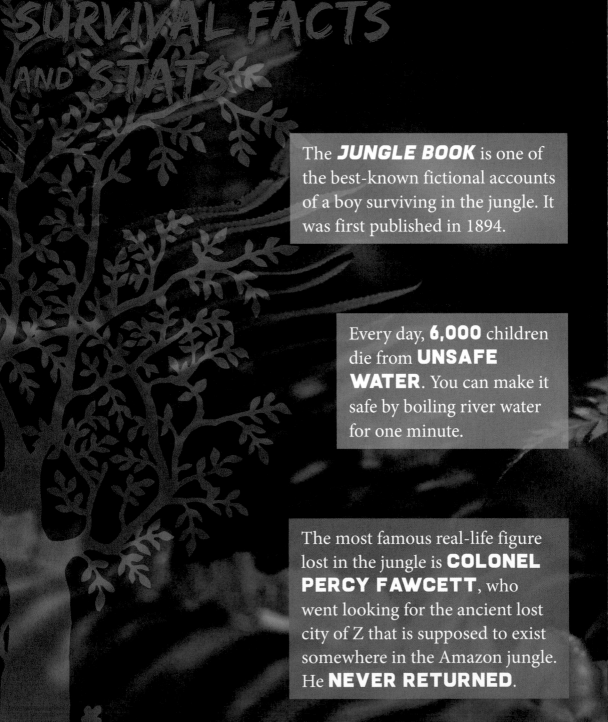

The **JUNGLE BOOK** is one of the best-known fictional accounts of a boy surviving in the jungle. It was first published in 1894.

Every day, **6,000** children die from **UNSAFE WATER**. You can make it safe by boiling river water for one minute.

The most famous real-life figure lost in the jungle is **COLONEL PERCY FAWCETT**, who went looking for the ancient lost city of Z that is supposed to exist somewhere in the Amazon jungle. He **NEVER RETURNED**.

Walking with a **STICK** hitting the ground in front of you can help scare dangerous **SNAKES** from your path.

To test if a **PLANT** is **EDIBLE**, you can rub it against your skin. If it makes your skin become red, itchy, or uncomfortable, it is likely unsafe.

Bugs that are **SAFE TO EAT** are the ones that are not brightly colored, do not have a strong smell, and are not large and hairy.

Most people lost in the jungle die from **POISONOUS** plants or unsafe water, and not animal attacks.

MAP

Some areas in the world are more dangerous than others. That is especially true in the jungle. Below are some of the most beautiful and dangerous jungles on Earth.

1. BORNEO RAIN FOREST

The Borneo rain forest is the largest rain forest in Asia. It is about 130 million years old. This is older than the Amazon. It is home to many different types of animals, including the pygmy elephant and the orangutan.

2. AMAZON

The Amazon spans 1.4 billion acres (566 million hectares) across South America. There is not much known about the area because it is so large and hard to navigate. The jungle is home to many dangerous animals and poisonous bugs.

3. SEONI JUNGLE

The Seoni Jungle was the inspiration for the *Jungle Book* and is located in India. It is also home to the Pench National Park and Tiger Reserve. Though there are many tigers in the area, the jungle is best known for its large herds of plant-eating animals.

4. ANCIENT WAIPOUA FOREST

Located in New Zealand, this jungle features massive Kauri trees. Some of the trees are 3,000 years old. Caves full of glowworms can also be found in this jungle. The worms twinkle with dim light.

IRON WILL

Many people who have been lost in the jungle do not live to tell their tale. The rain forest is thick with **vegetation**. The plants and trees are home to many types of dangers, from animals and insects, to fruit that can be deadly if eaten. In order to survive, people must be **resourceful**. If they know which plants and bugs are safe to eat, they can find food. They must also be alert and ready to spring into action if they see an animal or a snake. Moving toward civilization can help lead them to rescue. Many people move through the jungle on rivers. Staying near a river can help someone who is lost to be rescued. Most of all, survivors need the will to survive. Even when it seems hopeless, an iron will can make the difference between life and death.

vegetation: plants that grow in a certain area

resourceful: able to find solutions to problems or difficult situations

Having the right equipment and tools to survive in the jungle is important. The will to live is also equally important.

QUIZ

1 What accomplishment had Juliane Koepcke just celebrated before her plane crashed in the jungle?

2 What country are Loïc Pillios and Guilhem Nayral from?

3 How long was Yossi Ghinsberg lost for?

4 Who rescued Yossi Ghinsberg?

5 What did Gileno Vieira de Rocha eat to survive?

6 How old was Juliane Koepcke when she was lost in the jungle?

7 What kind of monkeys did Marina Chapman live with in the jungle?

8 How long did Marina Chapman think she lived in the jungle?

ANSWERS

1. Her high school graduation
2. France
3. Three weeks
4. His travel companion, Kevin Gale
5. Insects
6. 17 years old
7. Capuchins
8. Five years

ACTIVITY

Imagine you've been lost in the jungle. You have been lost with two or three travel companions. As a group, you must find a way to survive. Your teacher will provide you with the necessary supplies, some of which are listed below. Look at the survival tools on pages 36–37. Can you build or create any of these things with the provided supplies?

MATERIALS NEEDED

- construction paper
- scissors
- glue
- cardboard
- markers, crayons, or colored pencils
- additional art supplies (optional)

STEPS

1. Choose a survival tool to create: It will help your team survive!

2. Make a plan: Teamwork is key! Make a plan for how you will build your tool.

3. Assign tasks: Each member of the group should contribute to building your tool.

4. Work together: Use your assigned time to build your tool.

5. Compare and share: Share your tools with your classmates. What did they create? How would each tool help you to survive in the jungle?

GLOSSARY

bond: to form a relationship with someone

canopy: the topmost branges of trees in a forest, that form a layer of foliage above the forest floor

conscious: awake and aware of your surroundings

iron will: having a strong feeling that you are going to do something and that you will not allow anything to stop you

maggot: a small insect that looks like a worm; the young form of a fly

paralyze: to make an animal or human unable to move

parasite: an animal or plant that lives in or on another animal or plant and gets food or protection from it

preserve: an area where wildlife or natural resources are protected

remote: far from cities or populated areas

resourceful: able to find solutions to problems or difficult situations

terrain: a particular kind of land

underbrush: bushes, small trees, and other plants that grow under a forest's larger trees

vegetation: plants that grow in a certain area

venom: a poison that is inside of certain animals, such as insects and snakes, that can cause harm to humans or other animals

vulnerable: able to be easily attacked or hurt

READ MORE

Brazier, DJ. *Alone*. London, U.K.: Anderson Press, 2016.

Gallager, Belinda. *Jungle*. Survival Handbook. Essex, U.K.: Miles Kelly Publishing, 2014.

Long, David and Hyndman, Kerry. *Survivors: Extraordinary Tales From the Wild and Beyond*. London, U.K.: Faber & Faber Children's, 2017.

INTERNET SITES

https://kids.nationalgeographic.com/explore/nature/jungle/animal/
Jungle Animals

https://kids.nationalgeographic.com/explore/nature/jungle/
Explore the Jungle

https://www.coolkidfacts.com/jungle-facts/
Jungle Facts

INDEX